GOT FRUIT?

Practical Guide to Living Your Life Through The Fruit

Torre Lynn Adams

ISBN: 9781708978273

Merriam-Webster.com

torreadams68@gmail.com

Cover design: Torre Lynn Adams
Editor: Torre Lynn Adams

First Edition

Printed in the United States of America

FOREWARD

Got Fruit? This guide for living your Kingdom life the "fruitful" way, is a gem! Torre Lynn Adams, better known as "Peach" to many has released insight from her life journey about the importance of operating according to the Fruit of the Spirit.

The roux, the foundation, is and shall forever be love, and that message resounds throughout the writing. How do we as individuals navigate life without love? Honestly, we can't. We should love ourselves, love God and then allow the Holy Spirit to guide us as we continue walking in the Fruit of the Spirit in the workplace, with your family, your friends, your intentional and significant relationships, and in the church.

Whether you're a vegan, vegetarian, meat-eater or no eating preference at all, you'll need this dose of fruit, so get ready to eat up!

Apostle Valerie Burrell
Empowerment Place Ministries

PEACH ♡

I give honor to God, My Lord & Savior Jesus Christ, in whom I live & move & have my being. Thank you for saving me & shaping me. Peach ♡ to my grandmother, Albertine Adams, who embodied the Fruit, & walked upright before her children. Thank you for showing me what love looks like. Peach ♡ to my Mommy, the wind beneath my wings, thank you for teaching me how to fly. Peach ♡ to my dad, who showed me how a princess should be treated. Peach ♡ to my big sister, Monice, who is my biggest cheerleader. from the moment I mentioned I was going to write a book, she has pushed & pushed until it was done. You have never let me down, you little nut...lol Peach ♡ to my entire family, I love how you love me. Peach ♡ to Apostle Valerie Burrell (the General) for your support, your prayers, your sharpening. No longer am I ducking and weaving. I ain't scared. Peach ♡ to My Village, who support me, pray for me, love me, you all know who you are (my Pastor, Torre Young & St. John FREEWILL, M&M, SC4L, TCF, EP, Cuzn Pam, Cuzn Sheryl...) GET FRUIT Y'ALL

INTRODUCTION

Galatians 5: 22 *"But the fruit of the Spirit is love, joy, peace, longsuffering, kindness, goodness, faithfulness, 23 [g]gentleness, self-control. Against such, there is no law. 24 And those who are Christ's have crucified the flesh with its passions and desires. 25 If we live in the Spirit, let us also walk in the Spirit."*

I remember when I first began New Life Bible Institute in 2008, I had to do a presentation on the Fruit of the Spirit. Being a babe in Christ, sometimes the Word was a challenge to conceive and execute, but this seemed so plain. It has stuck with me since that time.

The bible tells us that as children of God, we are not of this world even though we are in it. As such, we ought not to conform to the things of this world. At times that's easier said than done. At times, if we're not careful, we can allow the film of the world to get on us, and we begin to resemble and act like it instead of looking like the Father.

God left his Word to instruct us on how to traverse our paths through this life. It's a great love story of redemption, but it is also a practical guide. The Fruit of the Spirit ushers us along through our travels and aids us in staying on the prepared road. It helps us treat one another the way God treats us.

If we are honest with ourselves, sometimes we are not feeling spiritual. Sometimes we are tempted to allow our flesh to flare for just a moment to handle some issue, but we can't lay aside our Spirit man because we're in our feelings. We have to be consistent in our presentation to the world. That's how we win souls.

This undertaking is an endeavor to provide tools that will help us stay focused on the plan God has for our lives, and not allow our will to supersede His, not even for a moment. There's work to be done, and His fruit will sustain us as we work. Beloveds, let's eat.

TABLE OF CONTENTS

FOREWORD BY: Apostle Valerie Burrell

PEACH ♡

INTRODUCTION

CHAPTER ONE - THE ROUX

"One of them, an expert in the law, tested him with this question: 'Teacher, which is the greatest commandment in the Law?' Jesus replied:'Love the Lord your God with all your heart and with all your soul and with all your mind.' this is the first and greatest commandment. And the second is like it: 'Love your neighbor as yourself. And the Law and the Prophets hang on these two commandments."
(Matt 22:35-40 NIV)

My family, like many in the late '50s and '60s, migrated north from the dirty south, attempting to escape blatant racism, and a quest to enhance their quality of life. In our case, they traveled from the bayou, Baton Rouge, Louisiana, that is. They brought along on their journey comforts of home that would make their new life a semblance of what they had left and loved. A staple that was included in many excursions, without taking up much room, were family recipes that were stored in the hearts and minds of those travelers.

Many a day during my childhood were spent at my grandmother's apron strings while she prepared our favorite down-home meals. Everything that Mother made was from scratch, ranging from her apple crumb cake (I still have her cake pan) and peach cobbler, shrimp and eggplant stuffed bell peppers, to everyone's favorite, her Creole seafood gumbo.

Like most of her counterparts, "Muh," as everyone called her, never used a written recipe. She made that gumbo so often; it was in her DNA. I'm confident she could prepare it in her sleep, and all of her grandchildren, I could tell you precisely how she did it step by step.

First, the chicken parts were to be skinned and browned in the frying pan. There were whole crabs, perfectly seasoned, and each shrimp meticulously deveined, or as she would say, "don't leave any black stuff down the spine."

Any proficient chef is aware that you have to cook that okra "just right," so it's not slimy. And lastly, but certainly, the most essential element was the roux.

Roux, pronounced "roo," is a mixture of flour and fat made on the stovetop that's used to thicken sauces or gravies. It's stirred until a golden brown hue — the darker the color, the greater the taste. The roux is the very staple of a perfect batch of gumbo. If you ruined it, you've ruined the entire recipe.

Now the makings of any great recipe, whether one follows a written prototype or it's etched in the rolodex of the mind, first prime ingredients. Start with the freshest of vegetables, meats, and spices. Secondly, after their separate preparation, it's all combined and simmered to perfection.

Even though Mother didn't use written recipes, the consistency in which she prepared the meal made it possible for her children to be able to recite it with ease. Her ingredients never changed; her preparation remained the same. She did all her measurements by sight, with the assurance it was accurate, and when the desired hue was attained, she knew it was pure perfection.

Just as in her food recipes, Mother left recipes for life as well. She left not a physical cookbook to keep up on the shelf with tattered pages to leaf through, held together by a rubber band or masking tape, but step by step by step, she embedded them where we could never be misplaced or forgotten. She jotted them down, as Proverbs 7:23 said, *"upon the table of our hearts."*

Every recipe begins with the main ingredient, the staple upon which the rest is built. That staple is love. It is the roux of the dish. It has been the roux of my life. My entire existence has been fueled by love, even before I knew it was fruit. Love propped itself up on the kitchen sink while I stood on a chair as Mother let me stir the gumbo pot. It took a seat and sat quietly while she and I dunked buttered toast into our morning cup of Maxwell House coffee (yes, coffee at five, don't judge my life).

Love never failed to make an appearance each and every time I fell and scraped my leg or got my feelings hurt. It scooped me up upon its lap and kissed every inch of my face. Love made me giggle while singing "Raindrops Keep Fallin' On My Head," even when the sun shined brightly.

See, love knew me before I knew love. And so it goes with God, He knew me before I knew Him. He loved me before I loved Him. His Word says He loved us before He even created the world. I didn't know that then, I just knew Mother. How was I supposed to know He loved her before she first loved Him. How did I know as a little Peach running up and down the street that she lived on was embodied by His Spirit and that everything that endeared me to her was because she ate from His fruit stand, and she liberally shared that fruit!

When I came into the knowledge of what love was, it's when I realized that the Apostle Paul was describing Mother in 1 Corinthians 13:4-5. Forever patient with us all, never tiring of the incessant noise that whirled around us like a swarm of honeybees, or the barrage of questions and requests for more, more, more, no matter what she doled out, we wanted more. There was a gentleness and kindness that exuded from her pores like those raindrops she sang about. She never crossed paths with envy, and humility left no room for boasting or pride to reside. Her thoughts were always to help others, give to others, forgive others. She only remembered the good of all. Here is where I realized what I was calling "Mother" was called "love."

Beloveds, it's not by happenstance that love is the first of the Fruit of the Spirit, for it's the element for which the remaining are hinged. After all, the Bible declares that it is the first and greatest commandment. And Jesus told us in John 13:34 to *"Love one another. As I have loved you, so you must love one another."* By this everyone will know that you are my disciples if you love one another." You cannot accomplish the sum and total of the Fruit absent love.

There's an old country song where the writer declares that he was "Looking for love in all the wrong places," and we, too, have found ourselves perusing the love aisle on countless occasions. We've come across a variety of brands in our search. Among the list, there's that Eros, that sexual, passionate one, the kind that can make you lose control if you're not careful. There's the "philia" flavor, which is that friendship bond with those who have endured alongside you. "Storge" love is how you love your family, your parents, your children. "Philautia," healthy self-love. It's the kind that allows you to accept and be comfortable in your own skin, unconditional love for yourself, which, in turn, will enable you to be able to love others.

Now, if you just tilt your head back and gaze your eyes upon the highest shelf in that love aisle, there, Beloveds, is where you will find the most supreme, the most satisfying, the most accepting, the all-consuming brand of them all, that is that "agape" love. It's the most pleasing to the palate, the sweetest of them all, never spoils; it just gets better with time. It's forever ripe, ready for consumption. You can never get enough, and it never runs out. It is the Love of God.

Agape love is the way our Daddy loves on us, and the way we ought to love on Him. It transcends our circumstances. It's the love that caused Christ to leave His heavenly throne, to endure suffering and persecution. It's the love that went to the cross for us. It's that John 3:16 love, "*For God so loved the world that He gave His only begotten Son, that whosoever believeth in him shall not perish, but have everlasting life.*" That's some love.

And because He loves us that much, it ought to cause us to love others in like manner. It ought to cause us to obey the second part of Matthew 22:39, "*love your neighbor as yourself.*" That's what He commands of us, and Beloveds, He put it in us to be able to do just that. And that commitment to God's obedience gives us the capacity to embody and implement, and it catapults us right into all of the other Fruits.

We were made in His likeness and image. We are His mini-mes in the earth. So that means if He loves, then we, too, can love. He left His Word to aid us in that very thing. His Word is a living organism, and when we allow it to live in us and direct our path, we can utilize its principles in a practical way to guide our lives, to enrich our lives, and to cause us to enrich and impact the lives of others.

Now you know how love became the roux of my life. Mother's love was like Psalm 133:2, "*It is like the precious oil poured on the head, running down on the beard, running down on Aaron's beard, down on the collar of his robe.*" That love was found at the end of those apron strings. That oil got on me, and it enables and empowers me to love as she loved, which is how He loved. That's the fuel of my life, it's working in me, and it, too, can work in you.

Just as Jesus invited the disciples to follow Him, love invited joy, peace, patience, kindness, goodness, faithfulness, gentleness, and self-control along its journey. When we allow the Holy Spirit to control our lives, we can possess these qualities. So, Beloveds, I invite you to journey with me as we learn to live our lives through the Fruit of the Spirit.

Amen.

2 LIVING YOUR LIFE IN THE FRUIT

We're living in a modern society where people feast on a regular diet of materialism and self-gratification, but there are those searching for a more fulfilling, palatable fare, one that will lead to a more satisfying and purposeful life. There is a recipe for success that can sate the appetite for those who desire a nutritional meal, one that will feed the mind, body, and soul. The good thing about this recipe, if you follow the directions below, it has an unlimited serving size, so there's plenty to go around. You can eat as much as you like; the more you consume, the healthier you will become.

We spoke in the previous chapter about the main ingredient, love. Love is all about action, Beloveds. Whether it be your family, your friends, even at work, it should be the cornerstone of your relationships. It should be the engine behind everything you do, every action you take. It's deliberate in its presentation, it affects the giver as well as the receiver. While you're busy loving everyone else, don't you dare leave yourself out of the equation. You can't possibly succeed in genuinely loving others if you have no love for you.

If, by chance, you are struggling with self-love, remember that He made you in His likeness and image. God doesn't make junk Beloveds, and if He loves you, He can't be wrong. You're loveable, and that's all there is to it.

Love or the lack thereof can affect one's health socially, physically, emotionally, spiritually, and intellectually. Oxytocin (not OxyContin, folks) is a natural hormone released in the body that's often called the love hormone. While it's more commonly referred to concerning a couple's love, it courses through our veins as we enjoy all whom we love; family, and friends. Love can affect one physically by assisting in lowering blood pressure, decrease stress and body aches, and increase energy. It can enhance intellectual and mental acuity and creativity.

Don't worry, this is not a science lesson, but it's imperative to understand the importance and the power that love possesses. Because when operating under love emotionally, intellectually, but most importantly, spiritually, you are more conscious of how you treat people, always building up and never tearing down. Love is other driven, not self-driven. It uplifts and honors, protects, forgives, and trusts. This kind of love is contrary to many worldviews today, but maintaining a positive and forward-focused outlook, you can cultivate a life that brims with joy.

The second ingredient, joy can't be found on just any shelf at your local market; it is homegrown. It is the ingredient that allows this recipe to be consumed hot or cold. This means you have joy not only in your mountain times but also in your valley experiences. Joy is hope in the throes of your life's tsunamis, allows you to believe that you will survive. It prevents you from looking like what you have been through. We cannot allow our negative experiences to override the positive. It is up to us to focus on the positive. For some whose habit it is to see the sad and wrong instead of the good, it may take some retraining, but it is possible. After all, Nehemiah 8:10 says, *"the joy of the Lord is my strength."* And with His strength, anything is possible.

When you have joy in your heart, it has an aroma of grace and peace that enters the nostrils of all around you. Peace, grace's partner, is an absolute must in a world where the behavior of "reality television" is spilling over into real life. There is a certain edge that seems to have permeated society, having many to believe the only way to succeed or accomplish their dreams and goals is by any means necessary, keeping others down, with aggression and yes, sometimes even violence. It's that mentality that I'm going to get you before you get me. Peace makes you allergic to drama. Possessing peace, an inner quietness, can enable you to control your environment. Peace is that soft answer, akin to using sugar, for instance, as a neutralizer to cut the acidity in some recipes. It can take the edge off, diffuse a situation.

Peace aids you in resisting the urge to respond in kind, an eye for an eye. You can remain calm, not react, but act thoughtfully and consistently.

Once you have combined your fruits, it is then time for baking. The temperature dial must be set on patience. Any other setting will fail. In this microwavable society, people want what they want the moment they want it, without waiting or working for it; but rushing leads to ruin. You don't want your favorite meal before the timer goes off. You don't want it half baked. That's nasty. The flavors of all the ingredients won't have time to mix and create your desired taste. You will have to put it back in until it's completely baked. The same thing is required with the things of God.

Patience is trusting that the plan God has for you is perfectly tailored for you, according to His time, not yours. There's a propensity to compare one's steps with those close to them. This can result in a deviation of the planned path God has for your life. It can even abort one's destiny. Making hasty decisions; in other words, decisions without seeking His will can lead to disaster. However, fostering patience will give one a clear portrait concerning personal goals instead of judging yourself against someone else.

It may seem that everyone around you is moving and prospering by leaps and bounds. It may seem like God has forgotten about you. It may seem like God even favors them more than He does you. Don't allow the enemy to mislead you. God is no respecter of person. He has no favorites. He loves us all, so much so that He crafted our path before we were even born. Psalm 139:13-16 (MSG) says, *"Oh yes, you shaped me first inside, then out; you formed me in my mother's womb. I thank you, High God-you're breathtaking! Body and soul, I am marvelously made! I worship in adoration—what a creation! You know me inside and out; you know every bone in my body; You know exactly how I was made, bit by bit, how I was sculpted from nothing into something. Like an open book, you watched me grow from conception to birth; all the stages of my life were spread out before you, The days of my life all prepared before I'd even lived one day."*

He has our life already mapped out. That's how faithful He is to His children. So we ought to be just as committed to Him and His will for ours lives. He has some good stuff in store for you as well, tailormade with your name on it. Tailormade with my name on it. So control yourself and your desire to get ahead of Him. Don't attempt to skip steps trying to keep up with the Joneses. If he wanted you to be like them, He would have made you a Jones.

Remember the game Simon Says? Simon says stop, Simon says move, that's how we ought to be with God. Don't you dare move until God says move. The Bible says it's not the swift who prevails, it's the one who endures, and might I add, the one who obeys. So, Beloveds, while you're waiting and obeying, please be gentle with yourself. We have a tendency to be quite hard on ourselves, harder than God is on us. He is a forgiving God, so let yourself off the hook; He has. Be kind to yourself; it will help you to be kind to others, which is His desire.

This life is a magnificent journey we are on with many mountains and valleys to traverse. Don't forget that the whole journey has already been mapped out for you, you just have to take the first step, and then another, and then another — one at a time. Jeremiah 29:11-13 tells us why, *"For I know the thoughts that I think toward you, saith the Lord, thoughts of peace, and not of evil, to give you an expected end. 12 Then shall ye call upon me, and ye shall go and pray unto me, and I will hearken unto you. 13 And ye shall seek me, and find me, when ye shall search for me with all your heart."*

So Beloveds, grab your fruit basket, you're going to need it for the journey.

3 WHAT'S FOR LUNCH –
FRUIT IN THE WORKPLACE

"OMG, that man is working on my last nerve like it's a banjo. He's so rude. He doesn't know how to talk to people. I have no idea how he got to be a manager. I don't care who he is, though, he is not going to talk to me like I'm one of his kids, because I'm not. I swear He's going to make me lay my religion down." "She is the worst employee I've ever had. I don't believe she has been on time for her entire tenure here. Then she gets an attitude if you ask her about it. Her work is not up to par, and she always has one excuse or another. I'm running out of patience with her for real."

Situations on the job will push you until you have had enough. They overwork you, underpay you, and only appreciate what you did for them ten minutes ago. Can you work late tonight? I know it's last minute, and your daughter's birthday is tonight, but this report has to be filed. I know I asked you to do it this way, but I've changed my mind, can you do it again." WHHHAAAATTTTT THE WHHHAAAATTTT !!!!

And then there's the little chick click in the department who's always keeping mess going. They spend half of the day gossiping about other people's business that they barely have time to complete their work by day's end. I'm so over this job and these people. Seriously, something or someone has got to change."

Question, "Have you ever found yourself in this predicament, fed all the way up with the work environment that you're busy reciting in your mind exactly what string of curse words are going to cut the deepest?" Sometimes it reaches the point where you understand why people go postal. You're not saying it's right, but you understand. If not, then you're better than me, because there have been times I made up some curse words I was so angry. So, instead of sinning, as Ephesians 4:26 says, I wondered was there an alternative. How, if at all possible, can you achieve harmony in the workplace instead of a termination notice or a visit to the local police department because you went completely off. The average American spends upwards of 57 percent of their waking hours on their "gig," more time than with their own family. Is it possible to create an environment that is conducive to a dual existence of harmony as well as high productivity?

Fear not, the good book provides the solution. After years of trying it my way, ways that most times did more harm than good, I've found that the remedy comes from, you guessed it, the Fruit of the Spirit. These nine gems function collectively as a single Biblical principle. They are a transferable skill that anyone can utilize, even in the workplace. However, the key to having the ability to function in them consistently is the Holy Spirit. The application of this distinctive method can combat acrimony amongst coworkers and help eradicate disharmony.

Let's face it; most of us have to work; there's no way around it. The Bible says in 1 Thessalonians 3:19 that *"The one who is unwilling to work shall not eat."* So, we have to grind, and it makes sense to create as much harmony as possible at our place of employment. One of our biggest mistakes is trying to deal with others in a like manner. Some can be adversarial, confrontational, and at times downright mean. There can be jealousy and unhealthy competition, as well.

Real talk, on occasion or two, that may have been you, may have been Torre Lynn.

What we don't realize is that when we do respond in kind, we are serving two different masters, two different bosses. While we are trying our best to do things God's way and we often fail, some aren't even trying. So it comes extremely easy to those who are not trying to please God to be underhanded. We really can't be mad at them, because they're acting like the boss they serve. They didn't profess Christ, you did. And when we react in kind, we are mimicking them instead of portraying our Father. We have to be obedient to who it is we serve. Admittedly some who have professed Him act more like those who haven't than those who do. And who we serve instructs us in Colossians 3:23 (NIV), *"Whatever you do, work at it with all your heart as working for the Lord, not for men."*

Yeah, yeah, yeah, Torre Lynn, sounds good, but how exactly do we accomplish this task? By embodying these virtues. Now, remember, they are the Fruit of the Spirit. That's the wonder-working power of His Spirit in you. Let the Spirit have its way.

And with the Spirit at work, self-control is at play. James 1:19 encourages *"every person to be quick to hear, slow to speak, slow to anger."* If we take the time to hear what someone is saying, what is the entire point before we respond, it is number one, a sign of humility, and number two, a sign of respect. You may not agree with them, but respect goes a long way. Being slow to speak allows God to direct your thoughts and bridle your first thought, which can sometimes come from an angry place, which never turns into anything good. So take your finger off of the reaction trigger. You don't always have to go toe to toe with them, nasty word for nasty word. Instead, you can do as Proverbs 15:1 advises that *"a gentle answer turns away wrath."*

We never want anyone to think we're a pushover, but whose opinion do we care most about, that chick on the job or your Father. This can be your secret weapon, the element of surprise. I'm not saying kiss up to them or be a pushover, but you don't have to be as nasty as they are either. You may be surprised at the change some of your coworkers may display, presenting a more gentle side of themselves, even if it's solely around you, or if nothing else, respect. Psalm 141:3

(NIV) tells us to *"Set a guard over my mouth, Lord; keep watch over the door of my lips."* This is what I call the Art of Silence, a/k/a "Going Mute." This is when you allow someone to complete their thoughts, and mute kicks in when after they have said their peace, but it was no peace in it at all, and your response would also be far from peaceful. So you lock your lips because you realize that's the safest for all involved. Guard your witness.

Now, there are times when silence doesn't seem too golden. It is then you may have to put into play THE ART OF WALKING AWAY, another form of self-control. We have to learn to pick our battles, and everything isn't a battle, it isn't. You don't have to prove yourself to everyone. Matthew 5:37 says to *"All you need to say is simply yes or no, anything beyond this comes from the evil one."* That's it, and that's all. Take your leave. Throw up the peace sign and be on your way. At times it is safer that way. Guard your witness.

Possessing Fruit can be akin to a domino effect. One will cause you to topple right over into the others. If you display love for all, your natural demeanor will radiate joy.

You know that one coworker who is always so pleasant and never without a smile or a kind word, that's that **un**speakable joy. She can bring the kinder side out of the most prickly person.

Romans 12:18 says that *"If it is possible, as far as it depends on you, live at peace with everyone"* Peace is that perpetual state of calmness. It can dictate how someone responds to you. Knowing you won't participate in drama will prevent the troublemakers from including you in their foolishness, and they will bypass your desk.

In an environment of coworkers complaining about the boss, gossiping about others, it's easier to assimilate in order to fit in. You can choose instead to be a light, allowing your sunny disposition to refocus conversations. You can also opt to excuse yourself from the situation.

Practicing patience and gentleness can be an art form, especially with those that can be a challenge with which to communicate. Functioning, for instance, in a supervisory position, can be a significant asset to high productivity.

As the boss, you deal with various personalities. It is your job to draw out their best work product. If you are looked upon as impatient, not understanding and unkind, you're going to find yourself in a perpetual battle of wills. Your subordinates won't go above and beyond for you; they may barely do the minimum.

We've all heard that teamwork makes the dream work. Well, that's true. So try not to create an atmosphere of them versus you. Instead, utilize your fruit. Be the kind of boss you would want. You get what you give. So plant plenty of seeds, you will reap a harvest of good.

Being a bearer of good fruit, upholding a moral standard of excellence, taking the high road, will influence those around you. A consistent display of these attributes will cause you to be an atmosphere changer, a harmonious atmosphere. When all is said and done, if you still possess a job and have avoided a prison stay, well then, you win.

4 FRUIT IN YOUR FAMILY

1 Peter 4:8 (NIV) "Above all, love each other deeply, because love covers over a multitude of sins."

Beloveds, we have entered our most challenging display of just how much fruit we possess, our family. Oh yes, indeed, this is where we put up or shut up, where the rubber meets the road, where your fruit will prove to be ripe from the tree or rotten to the core.

Our families are the group who have known us the longest, our entire lives. They are the ones who know everything about us; the good, the bad, and the ugly, the down dirty ugly. They are the people who know every button of ours to push and at precisely the right moment. Due to the intimacy of these relationships, these can be the ones that test us the most. We can tend to hold grudges longer, to be short-tempered and impatient, and at times unkind to one another. Unfortunately, we can also be the most judgemental with our families than we are with anyone else.

There are several familial relationships in the Bible that were fraught with drama; Cain and Abel, Jacob and Esau, Joseph and his brothers, and these are just in Genesis alone. I say that to point out that there is nothing new under the sun, they had issues as well.

We can, at times, treat our friends and others better than we treat those with the same bloodline. It's as if we have carte blanche to mistreat them and expect them to deal with it, to take it. God's word tells us to love everyone the same. He is no respecter of persons, and neither should we. Therefore, we ought to operate under the same virtues with them as we do others.

The best place to start, of course, would be with love. 1 Corinthians 13:4-8 (NIV) informs us that, *"4 Love is patient, love is kind. It does not envy, it does not boast, it is not proud. 5 It does not dishonor others; it is not self-seeking; it is not easily angered; it keeps no record of wrongs. 6 Love does not delight in evil but rejoices with the truth. 7 It always protects, always trusts, always hopes, always perseveres. 8 Love never fails."*

That's a mouthful, but if we could embrace and embody all that love is, we would do a lot better in our relationships with family. Parents lose patience with children, and it manifests itself in negative ways — arguments, accusations, name-calling, nothing that produces positive outcomes. The children don't hear what mom or dad is really saying because of the presentation. That can lead to anger, holding grudges, which is keeping a record of wrongs. That can lead to mistrust, mistreatment and the like.

Coming to the knowledge of Christ changes our very lives. The more we get to know Him and His Word, the more the old man in us should become less recognizable. We should begin to resemble more of Him and less of ourselves as we endeavor to do His will. This can be extremely challenging amid our family, especially with members who are not saved. Let's be real. It's as if we are always on display, waiting to fall so that they can point out our failures. How many times have you heard after making a mistake or did something you used to do, "I thought you were supposed to be a Christian." Now, that right there can certainly test your patience, most assuredly poke at your self-control, and cause you not to be so kind in your retort.

You may not want to hear this, but that's what you have to walk in, patience and self-control, in abundance. Why, because now you are not living for yourself, your life no longer belongs to you; it belongs to Christ. He paid a ransom for it, and it's now His will, not yours. You no longer get to respond in kind. Sorry. It's no longer about you; it's about Jesus.

We have heard it said that we are the only God that some people will see. So what are you showing your family about your God? Ask yourself that very question. Do you portray the fruits to them, or is your tree bare as far as they are concerned? Do you love them unconditionally or only when they do what you want? Do you promote peace at all costs, or do you delight in evil as the scripture above states? Do you speak gently and act kindly? Do you resemble Him at all?

This is our greatest training ground, our family. They can surely keep us humble because they know from whence we came. They know who we used to be, what we used to do, all our down and dirty. So who better to show that God has done a new thing in you. But here's the thing you are going to have to be consistent. The new you has to hold to that new standard. You can't curse them out Saturday night and praise the Lord Sunday morning without repenting, without apologizing, without admitting your mistake. That's not self-control...that's not patience....that's not living peaceably. Accepting when you're wrong, that's living upright before God, and before man.

Tramaine Hawkins sings, "A change, a change has come over me," and that's what we desire them to notice. We want them to see how powerful God is, that if he can change a hot mess like me, then he can change the hot mess that's in us all. Never losing sight of the fact that we were once them, and not that long ago, so we have to be patient with them. We were not changed overnight; it took time for us to be able to embody these fruits, to clothe ourselves in God's righteousness. And we can show that it's through His Spirit that we are made new. We can't ride around on a high horse looking down on them like we were born saved, because they know the real deal. They know we didn't change on our own. Let's be real; we don't possess the goods to pull this off on our own.

Allowing the Holy Spirit to reign in your life keeps you from being a hypocrite. It helps you to guard your witness. Keeping in mind that we want them to come to the saving knowledge of Christ as well, right? So we clothe ourselves in self-control, not popping off with our mouths when our buttons are pushed, not doing those things we used to do with them. Showing our faithfulness to God in all that we do is better than any lecture or sermon you can give. The more they see how you react gently to adversity, as opposed to the old you, that's going to go a long way with them. As you consistently a witness for Christ through your actions, not just your words, you will impact them, little by little, and you will hear less and less, I thought you were a Christian from them, and more and more well done from Daddy.

5 FRUIT WITH YOUR FRIENDS

12 *"Therefore, as God's chosen people, holy and dearly loved, clothe yourselves with compassion, kindness, humility, gentleness, and patience. 13 Bear with each other and forgive one another if any of you has a grievance against someone. Forgive as the Lord forgave you. 14 And over all these virtues put on love, which binds them all together in perfect unity."* **Colossians 3:12-14 (NIV)**

One of the vast ways that God has blessed me is in the area of friends. Many have come and gone in my life, but I have relationships that have spanned over four decades. That's no small fete for certain. Some began in early childhood, certainly before my knowledge and guidance of the Fruits at work. So this undertaking afforded me the opportunity, and prayerfully it will for you as well, to self evaluate my friend game. How do I measure up?

First, before the grading system begins, let's look at some things God says about friendship. Jesus, our greatest friend, commanded in John 15:12-15, *"This is my commandment, that you love one another as I have loved you. Greater love has no one than this that someone lay down his life for his friends."* Would I die for my friends? Would you? Proverbs 17:17 says, "A friend loveth at all times."....Do you love no matter what, or are there stipulations on your love? *"As iron sharpens iron, so a man sharpens the countenance of his friend." (Proverbs 27:17)* Do you strengthen your friend? Do you encourage your friend? *Philippians 2:4 ESV, "Let each of you look not only to his own interests but also to the interests of others."* Do you step out of your own little world to attend to the needs of others? *Galatians 6:2 ESV "Bear one another's burdens, and so fulfill the law of Christ.'* Do you have a heart connection? Are you bathed in compassion for them?

Certainly, there are many others, but these are a select few that can begin to lay out the blueprint of what a friendship should look like. And if you have these components, then your friend game is pretty tight. All of these being Godly principles, then the FOS can only serve to enhance and enrich and seal the bond.

Jesus has the tightest friend game EVER!! It's all fueled by His unwavering love for us. No matter what, He never stops loving us. Unlike Christ, we can, at times, be fair-weathered friends. Our friendship sometimes comes with stipulations, with ifs and thens; I will do this if you do that and only if. Our friendship sometimes has a schedule; we're only available like our gigs, 9:00 to 5:00, no weekends or holidays, and please don't call after 9:00. Our friendship can be like a rented vehicle with mileage restrictions; you live too far, cost too much to come and check on you.

At times some of us have the propensity to take our friends for granted. We nurture our relationship, prayerfully, with God. We continually work on our relationship, rightfully so, with our spouses. We even want to be more of a friend with our children, sometimes to their detriment, than their parents.

If we're not careful, this can lead to our friends falling by the wayside. We wake up ten or 20 years down the line and realize they're no longer there. Our children have flown the coop, and we're now an empty nester. Our spouse has a weekly golf game with the buddies, or she's off mall shopping with the girls. Suddenly there's a realization of how small our circle has become. Years earlier the friendship seed was planted; however, we neglected to regularly water it, let the sunshine upon it. Briefly, it sprouted but eventually faltered. It ceased to produce yearly fruit.

God created the bond of friends purposely. Remember, He's a relational God. That means they are just as important as all of our other relationships. They, along with our other relationships, help to complete us. God called Abraham his friend. David and Jonathan were best friends from their first meeting. The bible said that the soul of Jonathan was knit with the soul of David, and David loved him as his soul. They were committed to and supported one another through personal adversities in their lifetime. Although Jonathan's father, King Saul, attempted several times to kill David, it didn't destroy the bond of their friendship. It even spilled over to Jonathan's offspring. David loved his friend so much that he provided for his lame son, Mephibosheth, vowing that he would always eat at David's table and was treated like one of the family. David even returned the land of his grandfather, Saul, to Jonathan's son because of the love David had for Jonathan. That's a tight friend game.

Solomon explained the value of friends in Ecclesiastes 4:9-12 (NIV) 9 *"Two are better than one, because they have a good return for their labor: 10 If either of them falls down, one can help the other up. But pity anyone who falls and has no one to help them up. 11 Also, if two lie down together, they will keep warm. But how can one keep warm alone? 12 Though one may be overpowered, two can defend themselves. A cord of three strands is not quickly broken."*

Friends are the family you get to choose. Some of our friends are closer than our blood relatives. They are the "Village" that God gave us. Friends are like-minded people that support one another, as the Scripture above speaks. They show up when our siblings can't. Friends help out when our cousins won't. Friends answer when your spouse should, but doesn't.

One of my BFFs, Vette, and I have been rocking out for 40 plus years. In our teens, a situation occurred with several girls that had issues with me. I felt the matter could potentially become physical. So, when I told her about this, she came and had my back, by herself. Nothing physical occurred, but she showed me she was willing to put herself in harm's way for me. That one gesture sealed our bond for life. She showed her faithfulness to our friendship that day and every day since then. To this day I am confident she would fight a bear on my behalf. Her friend game is that tight.

If you are fortunate enough to possess a BFF like David, a ride-or-die like Solomon speaks of, someone who stands with you, that's the favor of God. Take this time to insert your own story of how your friend has gotten you out of a jam, stayed up and cried with you, went to bat for you, covered for you, paid that bill for you, prayed with you, prayed for you when you couldn't pray for yourself. Reread the chapter in your mind where they pulled you up when you were down, and yes, loved you enough to pull your coattails when you were a little too high on your horse for your own good.

What this trip down memory lane affords us is the ability to recognize how we ought to respond in kind, just what ought to dictate how we keep our friend game in good shape. Here is where we plug in Formula FOS. As a reminder, as we have established, these are godly principles. I'm in no way saying that we ought to treat unbelievers differently, for God is no respecter of person, and so we ought not be. However, we also should realize that if they aren't living for Christ, then their life isn't being dictated by His precepts. I said it previously, so you can't expect that person to be playing by the same playbook, God's Word, as you are. However, the opportunity is afforded us the ability to display His character through us. That can draw, that can teach, that can change people. After all, we are change agents in the earth.

One thing that we have to be careful with is labeling any and everyone as our "friend." Some folk are mere acquaintances, and we try to promote them to friend without first vetting them. What have they done to warrant the promotion? Please be extremely careful with who you invite into your inner sanctum. Even Jesus had a small circle, a circle of 12, and really three, Peter, James, and John, that were his inner circle.

That being said, what I have come to the knowledge of is that everyone's love language is unique. We show our love in various and sundry ways. So our relationships and the way we exist and operate in them should also be tailormade. No two people are the same, and thus no two relationships are identical. Our love for our friends should cause us to accept and embrace the differences in one another. Every facet of someone makes them who they are, and that's what propels us toward that person as a whole. The commonalities you have with someone are the draw, that's your foundation, your beliefs, your morals. Those things are the ties that bind.

Friends love you in spite of your shortcomings and all of your idiosyncrasies, just like Jesus. They allow you to be comfortable in your own skin. Their strengths cover your weaknesses. When you are embattled in all manner of war, just their gentleness with your tender heart can give you peace. They patiently listen as you pour out your broken heart to them, over and over again about the same subject, without judgment. They will honestly tell you that at this present moment you are a hot mess (not a judgment, but an observation), but they encourage you not to get weary because this here mess, this night season won't last always, but honey, morning is on its way and bringing with it joy.

A friend forgives you, just like God forgives you. He or she is not afraid to apologize for their mistakes, so neither should you. And they should be forgiven, just as God forgave us. A friend thought she hurt my feelings by something she said to me. Even though it did, I knew that because of our relationship, the hurt wasn't intentional. I trust my heart with her, so even if I felt some kind of way momentarily, I was able to get over that. I know her care for me wouldn't allow her to assault my spirit purposely.

Friendships, like any other relationship, are a work in progress. They are ever-evolving. You have to work to maintain the connection, the support that it provides. You have to nurture it as you would anything or anyone that you love. Friends sometimes are taken for granted and pushed aside, but the richness that they bring to your life adds to you being whole, complete and enriched.

God created the capacity of our hearts big enough to house love for friends. We see a lot of ourselves in them, and we also see in them things we wish we were. For example, I am someone who bears one another's burdens maybe a little too much at times. And depending on the situation, it can sometimes interrupt peace in my being. Two of the closest people to me in my life are my sister and my BFF, Monica, and Michelle, or M&M as I call them. They are my bookends. Their love game is so tight that in my mind, I really do think they can do anything. They make me feel like there's a force field around me because they have and continue to cover me. That's because they are faithful and committed to our bond.

Now what M&M don't possess is patience for any foolishness. Hear me when I tell you, none. They will do anything in this world for you, but never, never at the expense of their peace. It has taken me many years to arrive at the place that they are to be able to support someone without losing any of what's vital for me to stay centered. It's something that I admire about them. Boy would they fuss at me, but it's because they loved me enough to set me straight. What they had, they desired it for me. That's iron sharpening iron.

One thing I can honestly say is that they have always, always been gentle with my heart. They handle me with care. That's what we do to something we cherish; we take extra steps to ensure we don't allow it to be harmed. Your favorite sweater you hand wash with Woolite. Those limited-edition Jordans or Calloway golf clubs are treated like gold. Your favorite Louis Vuitton is always put back in the bag after use; Red Bottom shoes go back in the box, not under the bed. Handle with care.

Handling with care causes us to be patient with one another. We may not always like the things that our friends do, and they can't believe some of the foolishness we have done. We may not like the people our friends date or marry; they may be in a state of confusion at our choice of a mate, sometimes rightfully so. Handling with care will provide an extra measure of patience and self-control when we traverse challenges in those regards. Advice, criticism, opinions should be clothed in kindness and thoughtfulness. Even though we don't think they're the right choice, we operate in the fruit of self-control. Controlling what you say, and most assuredly, how you say it is paramount. And peep this, sometimes we should just say NOTHING. Sometimes the best thing to do is just to go mute. It might not be the time to shoot from the hip. For some, that's going to require an abundance of self-control. Resist the urge.

Hear me well; sometimes we want to get our point across so bad, we forget that this is someone we care for. We are good for saying, "You know, I just keep it real." We can't wait to say "I told you so, I knew he/she was no good," prove we know what we are talking about. We wield the smallest member of the body, the tongue, and do the most damage. James 3:5-6 (NIV) says about it:

5 *"Likewise, the tongue is a small part of the body, but it makes great boasts. Consider what a great forest is set on fire by a small spark. 6 The tongue also is a fire, a world of evil among the parts of the body. It*

corrupts the whole body, sets the whole course of one's life on fire, and is itself set on fire by hell."

You can prevent that forest fire by thinking about what it is I really want to accomplish by thinking before you speak. James 1:19-20 instructs *"My dear brothers and sisters, take note of this: Everyone should be quick to listen, slow to speak and slow to become angry, 20because human anger does not produce the righteousness that God desires."*

Ask yourself, do I just want to be right, or do I want to support my sister, my brother, in this situation? Do I react with my flesh so I can get the glory or allow God to get the glory by acting in a manner that ministers to my friend, that will help to restore them? Handle with care. How do we handle with care when a friend is wilding out, indulging in destructive behavior, straight tripping, a season of being a "hot mess." What do we do? What do we say when they are engaging in behavior that causes them to disrespect and dishonor themselves?

We, in no way, cosign their foolishness; no ma'am, no sir. The bible tells us in Galatians 6: 1-2, "Brothers and sisters, if someone is caught in a sin, you who live by the Spirit should restore that person gently. But watch yourselves, or you also may be tempted. **2** Carry each other's burdens, and in this way you will fulfill the law of Christ.

Take note the Scripture says gently. No browbeating, no finger-pointing, NO JUDGING, okay? That's not what they are in need of at that moment. Never forget that you, too, have come up short once, twice -- who are we fooling -- countless times, too many to remember; some we wish we could forget. You, too have made what looks like mistakes from which you can't recover. You made it, though. You have come through great trials, and you have endured, so you can tell them how you have come out. Your testimony can help them make it through their storms. You accomplish this with humility, not haughtiness, because you were once a hot mess as well. You accomplish this with compassion as well, because that's what your condition once required. So your job is to help them recover their footing when they stumble. Help them to stand again, stronger than before. In these moments, be gentle and kind with their wounded souls. Please, handle with care.

So, how's your friend game looking? Are you bringing you're "A" game? Are you operating in the FOS with your friends? Have some work to do? Can it be improved upon? Always. When you know better, you can do better. Let's do better by one another. Let's be a friend that loveth at all times. Let's handle one another with care. Friends share, so share your fruit.

6 FRUIT IN RELATIONSHIPS

"In the same way, you husbands must give honor to your wives. Treat your wife with understanding as you live together. She may be weaker than you are, but she is your equal partner in God's gift of new life. Treat her as you should so your prayers will not be hindered."
1 Peter 3:7

I know I said for better or for worse, for richer or poorer, in sickness and in health, to love and to cherish, till death do us part, but it sure seems like it's far worse than I could ever imagine, poorer than I believed anyone could be, so much sickness I forgot what health looks like, where is the love because I am not certain I can recognize it, and feeling cherished is a thing of the past.

There comes a time in many relationships where a variation of these sentiments are being felt. The love once cherished at times seem to be replaced by bitterness, resentment, unforgiveness. The love and joy you felt on that special day are but a fleeting memory. You don't even bother to look at the wedding video anymore, what's the point. It's like looking at a stranger when you do. That's not the person you married, no resemblance at all. Where there was once love, it is now hate. Joy has morphed into sorrow, and peace in the home is now replaced by a war of words, curse words you made up just for your mate. You think to yourself, 'This is not what I signed up for."

Well, what exactly did you sign up for? Did you plan the wedding down to the most minute of details but forgot to plan the marriage? Did you pull out all the stops to get a date, and as soon as you become comfortable, you ceased wooing? Did you have a game plan or consult a manual for what your relationship would be built on after all the pomp and circumstance had dissipated?

If you have ever been in just one romantic relationship in your life, then you know how challenging it can be. It takes real work. Work that takes a lifetime commitment. God ordained marriage from the beginning, in the very first book, Genesis, so it's important to him. So successful unions can and do exist, but you have to have a blueprint — what better guide than the Bible.

The Fruits are vitally important in a marriage. Your partner is the one you spend more of your time with than anyone in the most intimate ways; mind, body, and spirit. That leaves room for them to be the one which irks you more than others, who knows all of your buttons and can play them like they're tickling the ivories.

2 Corinthians 6:14 in the Message Bible records these words, "Don't become partners with those who reject God. How can you make a partnership out of right and wrong? That's not partnership; that's war. Is light best friends with dark? Does Christ go strolling with the Devil? Do trust and mistrust hold hands? Who would think of setting up pagan idols in God's holy Temple? But that is exactly what we are, each of us a temple in whom God lives. God himself put it this way: *"I'll live in them, move into them; I'll be their God, and they'll be my people. So leave the corruption and compromise; leave it for good,"* says God. *"Don't link up with those who will pollute you. I want you all for myself. I'll be a Father to you; you'll be sons and daughters to me."* The Word of the Master, God.

When I was in my twenties, I dated someone on and off for many years. He was who I thought would be "the one" eventually. During one of our year or two long breakups I got serious about my walk with God, and he embraced another faith. It was extremely difficult to walk away from him because we had such a strong connection.

However, as I began to grow, I realized just how important being equally yoked was. While our physical relationship was fantastic, we now had a different doctrinal foundation. That would have wreaked havoc on both of us because we would always be jockeying for position, debating about whose beliefs were right, someone eventually succumbing to the pressure and compromising who and what they stood for. As heartbreaking as it was, we had to walk away.

So, you see, the love that both of you have for God is going to be the common denominator. You both made a covenant with God, and you made a covenant with one another when you stood before him and made a vow. You both have His spirit reigning in your life; that's how the Fruits can take root in your relationship. You two are working towards the same things. You're teammates, and what do teammates do, they build one another up, encouraging them because you all have the same goals.

Ephesians 5:**25 says,** "*Husbands, love your wives, even as Christ also loved the church, and gave himself for it.*" If you love your mate like Christ loves the church, then you will always have his/her best interest at heart. You won't take them for granted. You get joy just making them happy. 1 Peter above tells the husband to honor her and treat her with understanding. Now that doesn't always mean you're going to understand her, because admittedly we are beyond understanding at times, but you should endeavor to understand. And when you don't, approach her with gentleness and kindness. She's not your enemy; she's your friend, she's your lover. Remember that when tensions arise.

Men, calm down, I know there's a mandate on her as well. Ephesians 5:**22-23,** *"Wives, submit yourselves to your own husbands as you do to the Lord.* **23** *For the husband is the head of the wife as Christ is the head of the church, his body, of which he is the Savior."* Men love this scripture; women not so much. The biblical meaning differs from the world. The world automatically thinks this means that they are going to boss us around like slaves and that we have no rights. This is why it's essential to be equally yoked. If you, husband, are following and obedient to Christ, then your mission is never to dishonor or disrespect your wife. She's following you as you follow Christ. And if you are following Christ, then you ought to love her with the love of Christ. You don't dishonor or disrespect, enabling her the ability to submit. Remember God's grace toward you, and then extend that same grace to your mate.

Those who may be married and saved but your spouse isn't, the Fruits still apply. You are not off the hook with practicing them. It's still a mandate for you. Your consistency operating in them could be the very thing that brings them to the knowledge of Christ. Keep planting and watering that seed; God will increase it.

Coming together as one takes diligence and patience. You're not going to always agree, but there's a way to achieve harmony. You have to operate in patience and self-control - you have to. Everything we do is supposed to bring God glory. I said it before when we dishonor one another; we are dishonoring Him.

Hush up for just a moment, and listen. Control your tongue, watch how you wield it because once you cut someone, they're going to bleed. You know it's a two-edged sword. Why do we intentionally draw blood from those we say we love? You can say what you feel, your opinion, absolutely, but how are you serving it? Are you calm when you speak? Are you remembering this is the love of your life because, at times, you go at one another like mortal enemies? Take off your armor, put it down, because the war is not with one another, it's with the enemy who wants to see you at battle.

Now, this kind of behavior is adverse to the worldview of I'll get you before you get me. However, we are in this world, but not of it. We don't get to play by their rules, because our Ruler has laid out instructions on how we traverse life. We have to represent Christ no matter what we face. Your marriage can be an example of how it can be successful when we allow Christ to be the head of our lives. You walk upright before your friends, husband, and show your friends how to be faithful to their wives. You, his queen, can provide a peaceful atmosphere at home with your patience when he doesn't do things exactly the way you like. Don't sweat the small stuff. Everything doesn't have to be a battle.

I don't want you to think I'm living in la-la land. I know life isn't a sitcom. I'm not naive, but I am practical.

Life happens, and sometimes it happens big and bad and ugly. Sometimes it's unkind and can be so devastating that it takes your breath away. These are the times when your helpmate and you can be strong because you function as a single entity. You have nurtured one another and always esteemed the other higher than yourself, which is what Ephesians 4:32 encourages us to, **32"** *Be kind and compassionate to one another, forgiving each other, just as in Christ God forgave you."*

Your bond can become impenetrable, and that's because you trust one another with your heart. You have proven your love and devotion because of the way you have consciously treated one another. You have made a conscious decision to allow God to direct your paths, as Proverbs 3:5-6 instructs. I mentioned in an earlier chapter that a cord of three strands is not quickly broken. That three-strand cord is God, you and your mate. He is the one in the middle that binds the others to Himself, that way you're not easily unraveled. Stick and stay close, hold onto Him and His spirit will continually nourish you with the Fruit of the Spirit, more than enough for the journey.

CHAPTER SEVEN- FRUIT IN THE CHURCH

"As we have therefore opportunity, let us do good unto all men, especially unto them who are of the household of faith."
Galatians 6:10

"I thought you were supposed to be saved." She's acting just like the world." One would just assume that church folk operated in the Fruits. I mean, after all, we are talking about the attributes of our Saviour activated in us through His Spirit. Just seems obvious, a no-brainer. One would think. One would think that we would at least treat our own brothers and sisters in the Lord with love. After all, we take the time to get dressed for Sunday worship, wearing our finest, supposedly presenting our best for the Lord, but in actuality wanting to impress man. We make certain we have all of our Jesus paraphernalia; bible, cross and the like. We sing on the Praise and Worship team, but there's no praise in our hearts and no real worship in our spirit.

1 Corinthians 12:12 "Just as a body, though one, has many parts, but all its many parts form one body, so it is with Christ". We forget at times that we are of the same body, the

body of Christ. When we dishonor one of our siblings in the faith, we dishonor our Father. We dishonor ourselves. Would you purposely put your own hand to the fire? Would you take a bat to your own leg and break it? Why then would you harm your brother or sister? What benefit is that to you? What benefit is that for the body of Christ? That handicaps the body if any of the members are not functioning. What benefit is that for unbelievers who view that manner of behavior?

Lest we not forget that our mandate in Matthew 28:19-20 is to go out into all the world and spread the gospel of Jesus Christ, to show the love of He who sent us, and to make disciples. Who are we attracting with our behavior toward one another? We wonder why the church isn't growing, it's because our love is tainted, like spoiled meat. Who is that appealing to? Who wants to feast on that? I submit to you, no one.

In John 13:34, Jesus instructs us saying, " A new commandment I give to you, that you love one another: just as I have loved you, you also are to love one another. 35 By this all people will know that you are my disciples, if you have love for one another."

This is not a suggestion, this is a commandment. Love. And we ought to love who he loves. After all, it's with his Spirit that we can accomplish this. Remember that's the power that enables us to mirror Him. His spirit is the engine that powers us. It's an ever-working engine, you should not be hitting the on and off switch when you don't feel like being spiritual. It's not about you. The Holy Spirit has a work to do, so let him do that which He was sent to do.

That very engine is what activates the Fruits within us. We need that to traverse this world and the people therein, even God's people. Because even though we are not of this world, we have to live in this world. And sometimes God's people mirror this world. That's real talk. Sometimes you and sometimes I can get real funky with one another. Even though we are supposed to be like-minded, we aren't always on the same page. We don't always get along. We have issues with one another. Sometimes we are just hard to love, but hard doesn't mean impossible. We need a reminder of who we belong to and who we represent.

Colossians 3:12-17 12Therefore, as God's chosen people,

holy and dearly loved, clothe yourselves with compassion, kindness, humility, gentleness and patience. 13Bear with each other and forgive one another if any of you has a grievance against someone. Forgive as the LORD forgave you. 14And over all these virtues put on love, which binds them all together in perfect unity. 15Let the peace of Christ rule in your hearts, since as members of one body you were called to peace. And be thankful."

The love we have for Christ, which then extends to our kinfolk, should always be the barometer we use, not our own. Would you curse Christ out? Well, then how can you curse your pastor out? How can you sit next to a co-laborer in the same pew, and not even speak? Would you ignore Christ? He's no respecter of person, and you shouldn't be either. They were born in sin and shapen in iniquity, and just in case you forgot, so were you. So the patience that was afforded you after you messed up for the umpteenth time, you better take a deep breath, count to ten and then extend that same grace.

Increasingly the church is beginning to resemble more of the world than it should. We are bringing too much of their ways into the church, when it should be the converse, we should be taking the church into the world. What I mean by that is we can't operate under their rules: curse me out, I curse you out; hate me, I hate you back. We can't solve our differences like them.

We operate in the world the same way they do, and then it becomes increasingly difficult to put on our saved and sanctified hat on Sundays. That worldly spirit begins to seep into our relationships with the Saints. We have to be consistent in our character. If we operate by the Spirit no matter where we are and who we are around, saved or unsaved, we won't be confused. Maintaining integrity is a Godly characteristic. That will win souls, your consistency. People will recognize that essence as different, but attractive.

Remember that we are of the same household, the household of faith. That should mean something to us. We shouldn't want to be in conflict with one another. We should have one another's best interest at heart. Our will should line up with God's will. He would have us to be whole, we should want that for one another, which leads us to wanting it for all. After all, we should be about Kingdom business, our Daddy's business. That is increasing His household of faith.

Matthew 9:37 tells us that the harvest is plentiful, but the workers are few. That means we're all needed for this work. It's time out for playing, souls are on the line. We have to showcase all the virtues of Christ to the world to draw them unto Him. So Beloveds, we start at home, with one another. Love one another with the love of Christ. Do your best to bring joy to your colaborers. Do everything in your power to live peaceably and promote peace. Walk in peace, dispense it everywhere your foot treads. Give the gift of patience and kindness to this dying world, for it will be welcomed and cherished. Do good that man might see and glorify your Father in heaven. Be faithful, for the Bible says that he that is will abound in blessings. Your gentleness with other's will soothe their souls and draw them to God's heart. That is our ultimate goal, to please our Daddy, and draw souls to Christ.

Beloveds, there are benefits for doing a good job to bearing fruit. They are "that you will walk in a manner worthy of the Lord, to please Him in all respects, bearing

fruit in every good work and increasing in the knowledge

of God." as recorded in Colossians 1:10.

The benefit Hebrews 12:11 tells us about is that "All discipline for the moment seems not to be joyful, but sorrowful; yet to those who have been trained by it, afterwards it yields the peaceful fruit of righteousness".

Psalm 92:13-14 tells us of lasting fruit, "Planted in the house of the LORD, they will flourish in the courts of our God. They will still yield fruit in old age; They shall be full of sap and very green."

Matthew 13:23 says "And the one on whom seed was sown on the good soil, this is the man who hears the word and understands it; who indeed bears fruit and brings forth, some a hundredfold, some sixty, and some thirty." That's a benefit of great quantity.

Psalm 1:3 He will be like a tree firmly planted by streams of water, Which yields its fruit in its season And its leaf does not wither;" and the benefit is that in whatever he does, he prospers." Now that's a great benefit.

My prayer, Beloveds, is that you have been encouraged in your walk with Christ to embody his characteristics as you show up in the world. We are His representatives, after all, and we want our "light to shine before others, that they may see your good deeds and glorify your Father in heaven." Continue to be led by His Spirit, and you will surely be able to answer yes when asked if you've "GOT FRUIT."

ABOUT THE AUTHOR

Minister Torre Lynn Adams hails from Philadelphia, Pennsylvania, where she has been a life-long member of the St. John Freewill Baptist Church. She has been under the leadership of Pastor Torre Young since 2011.

Torre Lynn obtained an Associate's of Science degree from Manor College, where she studied court reporting and has been in the field for over 30 years.

She graduated from the New Life Bible Institute in 2014, where she presently serves as an instructor. She also received a Bachelor's in Religious Education from the United Christian Fellowship Theological Seminary, the Philadelphia

Campus of the Eastern Theological Seminary headquartered in Lynchburg, Virginia. She completed and received a Master's in Theology in 2019 from the same institution. She also serves on their teaching faculty.

Her life's scripture is Proverbs 3:5-6, *"Trust in the Lord with all thine heart; and lean not unto thine own understanding. In all thy ways acknowledge Him, and He shall direct thy paths."*

Minister Adams has a heart for God's people, especially his daughters, where she seeks to educate, edify, and encourage them in traversing their life's journey to becoming all the Father created for them. Her only desire is to do the will of the Father...that's it, and that's all.

CONTACT: torreadams68@gmail.com

Made in the USA
Middletown, DE
10 February 2020